**CCSS** **Genre** Fiction

MW00479641

 Essential Question
What do we love about animals?

Alice's New Pet

by Anita Rodriguez
illustrated by Ruth Flanigan

Chapter 1
A Kitten?

Alice cleared her throat. Her mom was sprawled on the sofa. She was lost in a book. "Mom, I need a pet," Alice said.

Her mother barely looked up. They had been through this before. "You *need* one?"

"Yes, so I can do my homework," Alice said.

"Really?" Mom sat up. She looked amused. "Just where do you think we'll find a pet that can do second-grade math?"

Alice groaned. She liked Mom's jokes, but this was serious.

"I need to write a poem about an animal," Alice explained. "I can't use pictures or books. I have to watch it move, sleep, and eat. I need to see how it lives. So we should adopt a kitten!" Alice really wanted a kitten.

Mom ignored Alice's request for a kitten. "But you can write about any animal, right?" she asked.

"Yes, if I can watch it long enough to write about it," Alice said.

"How about a poem about a bird?" Mom pointed out the window.

Chapter 2
A Bird?

A plump robin sat on a telephone wire. It tucked its head under a brown wing. Alice noticed bright orange feathers on its chest. The tiny beak was a dull yellow.

"Maybe I really can write a poem about this bird," she thought.

Alice picked up her pencil and said,
"I can call my poem *Robby the
Robin*." She thought about what it
must be like to spread wings and fly.

She imagined Robby saying, "Flying
makes me feel strong and free!"

6

Suddenly, the robin was flapping its wings. It zoomed through the air.

"Oh, no! It's gone!" Alice said.

"You'll find another," Mom said.

Alice looked down at her paper. She scribbled over the few words she had written on the page.

"How will I see how birds behave if they fly away before I can get a good look?" Alice asked. "Can't we just get a kitten? It would be so much easier."

"You know how your brother sneezes
and coughs around cats," Mom
answered. She rose from the couch.
"There are plenty of other animals
outside. Let's go for a walk."

Chapter 3
A Bug!

It was a warm spring afternoon.
Plants had begun to sprout. Alice
carried her notebook and pencil. She
was ready to write. Maybe she could
borrow a neighbor's dog.

Alice tried to think of other places to see animals. "We could go to the zoo," Alice said. "Then I could write about a lion." Alice tried to imagine how a lion would express itself. "I am the fierce and mighty king of the jungle!" it would roar.

"We don't need to go to the zoo to
find animals," Mom said. "There are
animals all around." She pointed to
a bunny scrambling to hide behind
a tree. She squeezed Alice's hand.
"Don't worry. You'll find an animal
to write about."

Alice looked down at the sidewalk. A large green bug was heading toward the grass.

"A bug is a kind of animal!" Alice said to Mom.

But what could she say about a bug? She loved to look at bugs, but this was just a plain old beetle.

Alice bent down to look closer at the little bug. What would it say about itself? She imagined the bug would speak in a scratchy voice.

It would say, "I may be small, but look at my back! My hard shell defends me from hungry birds who want snacks."

"I have something that might help you," Mom said. She pulled a small glass jar from her purse.

"How did you know?" Alice asked.

Mom smiled. Alice carefully put the bug in the jar. She added three small twigs so the bug would feel at home.

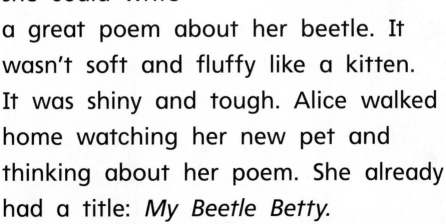

Alice knew she could write a great poem about her beetle. It wasn't soft and fluffy like a kitten. It was shiny and tough. Alice walked home watching her new pet and thinking about her poem. She already had a title: *My Beetle Betty.*

Respond to
Reading

Summarize

Use details
to summarize
Alice's New Pet.

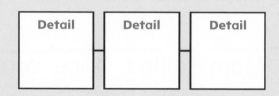

Text Evidence

1. How do you know that *Alice's New Pet* is fiction? Genre

2. What does Alice need to do for homework? Use details from the story. Key Details

3. What does *sprout* mean on page 10? Use context clues to figure it out. Multiple-Meaning Words

4. Write about Alice's problem and how she solves it. Include details in your answer. Write About Reading

Compare Texts
Now read a poem about another lovable animal.

Baby Joey

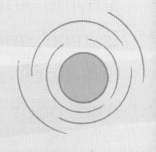

A jumping, bouncing kangaroo
Has a baby who's brand new.
In her pocket Joey rests,
Safe and snug in his warm nest.

Much too small to see the world,
In Mama's pouch, he stays curled.
Sipping milk to make him strong,
For nine months he rides along.

Staying safe in Mama's pouch
Is nice and cozy like a couch.
But Baby Joey wants to play
And pops out his head one day.

Once upon the forest floor
Joey sets out to explore.
He thumps his tail and with a "pop!"
Little Joey starts to hop!

Make Connections

What does Alice love about bugs?

Essential Question

How is Baby Joey like the animals in *Alice's New Pet*? Text to Text

Focus on
Literary Elements

Rhythm Poems have rhythm, or a pattern of beats. Stressed beats are said with more force. Unstressed beats are said with less force.

What to Look for In this poem, the stressed beats are in **bold** letters.

Sipping **milk** to **make** him **strong,**
For nine **months** he **rides** a**long**.

Try reading the lines above out loud.

Your Turn

Write a short (4-line) poem. Your poem can rhyme, or not. Say your poem a few times to yourself or out loud. Identify the stressed beats. Underline them.